TECHNICAL BIBLIOGRAPHIES ON AGING

ETIOLOGY OF MENTAL DISORDERS IN AGING: A SELECTED BIBLIOGRAPHY

Edited by:
Arthur N. Schwartz, Ph.D.

ETHEL PERCY ANDRUS GERONTOLOGY CENTER
UNIVERSITY OF SOUTHERN CALIFORNIA
UNIVERSITY PARK
LOS ANGELES, CALIFORNIA 90007

This publication was supported in part by two grants from the U. S. Administration on Aging: Foundations for Research in Social Problems of Aging 93 P 57621/9-01 and Integration of Information on Aging 93 P 75151/9-02.

ISBN 0-88474-022-6

© 1975

Published by:
Office of Publications and Media Projects
Richard H. Davis, Ph.D.
Director

Richard Bohen
Bibliographies Project Director

Claudette Culbreath
Editorial Assistant

THE UNIVERSITY OF SOUTHERN CALIFORNIA PRESS

CONTENTS

Pages

I. GENERAL MENTAL HEALTH 1

II. GENERAL MENTAL DISORDERS —
INCLUDING SENILITY 4

III. GENERAL GERIATRIC PSYCHIATRY 21

IV. ORGANIC BRAIN SYNDROME 25

    A. Chronic Brain Syndrome 25

    B. Alzheimer's Disease 26

    C. Assessment 27

V. PSYCHOSES 29

    A. General 29

    B. Manic-Depressive 33

    C. Schizophrenia 34

    D. Paranoia 37

    E. Regression 38

VI. NEUROSES 39

    A. General 39

    B. Depression — Including Hysteria 40

VII. AFFECT 48

    A. Affective Changes With Age 48

    B. Anxiety, Agitation, and Tension 49

VIII. MENTAL CONFUSION 50

FOREWORD

This is a selected bibliography of references taken from a keysort file of 45,000+ references. This file is established in the Andrus Gerontology Center, compiled from commercially-available data bases and published sources relevant to gerontology. The data bases consisted of BA Previews *(Biological Abstracts* and *BioResearch Index)*, MEDLINE/MEDLARS *(Index Medicus)*, PASAR *(Psychological Abstracts)*, Drug Abuse Information Center, Brain Research Information Service, *Sociological Abstracts* (1963-1967), *International Political Service Abstracts*, ERIC, NTIS and NEXUS. The published sources were primarily compiled from the entire file of Dr. Nathan Shock's "Current Literature in Gerontology and Geriatrics" published in each issue of the JOURNAL OF GERONTOLOGY, from 1959-1974 and various announcement services, such as PUBLISHERS' WEEKLY, MONTHLY CATALOG OF U.S. GOVERNMENT PUBLICATIONS, MONTHLY CHECKLIST OF STATE PUBLICATIONS, DISSERTATION ABSTRACTS, etc. All references were originally entered into the keysort file without editing or checking.

For this bibliography, all references of questionable accuracy were checked or deleted as the verification process was performed. Most of the references were selected from 1959-1974. However, some earlier ones were included if they were regarded as significant in the area of study. English-language references were stressed in the selection criteria but foreign titles containing unique data were not excluded. In many cases the titles have English abstracts for the convenience of the reader.

Many of the references listed herein can be obtained through a library or the interlibrary loan system. They are not necessarily available from the Andrus Gerontology Library at the University of Southern California. In some cases, the books may still be in print and can be purchased through a local bookstore or jobber. For journal articles, the full name of the issuing journal has been spelled out to aid in the acquisition of the item through their own library.

We wish to thank the bibliography staff for their help in making this bibliography possible.

Julie L. Moore, Project Bibliographer	Kristen Eisenhart
Barbara H. Johnson, Project Assistant	T. Pong Hee
Gary A. Baffa	Elizabeth Zelinski
Kathleen L. Culbertson	

I. GENERAL MENTAL HEALTH

Ando, H., Hasegawa, E., & Ogawa, I. (A study on the mental hygiene states of the aged; comparative surveys in a big city, a mountain village and an asylum for the aged.) *Psychiatria et Neurologia Japonica,* 1969, *71,* 492-505; 524-525. (*Biological Abstracts,* 1970, *51,* 43254.)

Anonymous. (Various problems of mental hygiene in the aged.) *Journal of the Japanese Medical Association,* 1964, *49,* 133-146.

Balier, C. Hygiène mentale et vieillissement. In F. Bouliere (Ed.), *Progrès en gérontologie.* Paris: Éditions Médicales Flammarion, 1969, 331-349.

Braceland, F. J. The mental hygiene of aging: Present-day view. *Journal of the American Geriatrics Society,* 1972, *20,* 467-472.

Butler, R. N. & Lewis, M. I. *Aging and mental health; positive psychosocial approaches.* St. Louis: C. V. Mosby, 1973.

Clausen, J. A. Conceptual and methodologic issues in the assessment of mental health in the aged. *Psychiatric Research Reports,* 1968, *23,* 151-160.

Davies, G. V. Analysis of the mental health of older women in Australia. In C. Tibbitts & W. Donahue (Eds.), *Social and psychological aspects of aging.* New York: Columbia University Press, 1962, 628-631.

Eaton, M. T., Jr. The mental health of the older executive. *Geriatrics,* 1969, *24,* 126-134.

Gillet, J. A. Mental health of the elderly. *Journal of the Royal Institute of Public Health,* 1967, *30,* 78-82.

Hacker, S., Gaitz, C. & Baer, P. Residence as a factor in the mental health of the elderly. *Proceedings of the Gerontological Society,* 1967, *20,* 39.

Hansen, G. D. *Mental health and aging in Oregon.* Mount Angel: Oregon Gerontological Study and Training Center, Mount Angel College, 1965.

Hoch, P. H. & Zubin, J. (Eds.) *Psychopathology of aging.* New York: Grune and Stratton, 1961.

Hoff, F. (Defense mechanisms of the organism.) In W. Doberauer (Ed.), *Scriptum geriatricum.* Vienna: Gesellschaft f. Geriatrie, 1972, 19-35.

Kent, D. P. Social and cultural factors influencing the mental health of the aged. *American Journal of Orthopsychiatry,* 1966, *36,* 680-685.

Khatun, S. Mental hygiene in old age. *Pakistan Journal of Geriatrics,* 1967, *5,* 9-10.

Krapf, E. E. Family mental health and the older generation. *Public Health Papers of the World Health Organization,* 1965, *28,* 90-94.

Lowenthal, M. F. The relationship between social factors and mental health in the aged. *Psychiatric Research Reports,* 1968, *23,* 187-197.

Marmor, J. The crisis of middle age. In G. Usdin (Ed.), *The psychiatric forum.* New York: Brunner/Mazel, 1972, 33-38. (*Psychological Abstracts,* 1973, *49,* 5241.)

Meltzer, H. & Ludwig, D. Age differences in positive mental health of workers. *Journal of Genetic Psychology,* 1971, *119,* 163-173.

Mizrukhin, A. I. (Clinical picture and course of psychogenia in middle and old age.) In N. B. Mankovsky (Ed.), (*Problems of experimental and clinical gerontology.*) Kiev, U.S.S.R.: Academy of Medical Sciences, 1968, 135-136.

Moriwaki, S. Correlates of mental health in an aged population: An analysis of supported self-disclosure. Unpublished doctoral dissertation, University of Southern California, 1971.

Morris, W. W. (Ed.) Mental health of the older adult. *Proceedings of the University of Iowa's eleventh conference on gerontology.* Iowa City: Institute of Gerontology, University of Iowa, 1966, 1-125.

New York State Department of Mental Hygiene. Mental Health Research Unit. *A mental health survey of older people.* Utica, N.Y.: State Hospitals Press, 1961.

von Rappard, I. Psychohygiene des Alters. *Proceedings of the 7th International Congress of Gerontology.* Vienna: Wiener Medizinischen Akademie, 1966, *8,* 599-602.

Rose, A. M. Mental health of normal older persons. In A. M. Rose & W. A. Peterson (Eds.), *Older people and their social world.* Philadelphia: F. A. Davis, 1965, 193-199.

Schwarz, H. (Mental hygienic tasks in old age.) *Deutsch Gesundheitswesen,* 1967, *22,* 2342-2345.

Weinberg, J. Mental health in the aged. In M. M. Dacso (Ed.), *Restorative medicine in geriatrics.* Springfield, Ill.: Charles C. Thomas, 1963, 259-274.

White House Conference on Aging. *Section recommendations on physical and mental health; with related recommendations from other sections and Special Concerns Sessions.* Washington, D. C.: U. S. Government Printing Office, 1972.

Yap, P. M. Aging and mental health in Hong Kong. In R. H. Williams, C. Tibbitts & W. Donahue (Eds.), *Processes of aging. Volume II.* New York: Atherton Press, 1963, 176-191.

II. GENERAL MENTAL DISORDERS – INCLUDING SENILITY

Aaronson, B. S. Aging, personality change, and psychiatric diagnosis. *Journal of Gerontology*, 1964, *19*, 144-148.

Agresti, E. & Ballerini, A. (Contribution to the study of the delusions of the involutional age.) *Giornale di Psichiatria e di Neuropatologia*, 1961, *89*, 829-884.

Akimoto, H. (Problems on mental disorders in old age.) *Iryo*, 1968, *22*, 1131-1137.

Anderson, C. J., Porrata, E., Lore, J., Alexander, S. & Mercer, M. A multi-disciplinary study of psychogeriatric patients. *Geriatrics*, 1968, *23*, 105-113.

Anderson, J. F. A study of disturbed behaviour in patients with dementia in two hospital populations. *Gerontologia Clinica*, 1970, *12*, 49-64.

Anderson, R. J., Price, A. C. & Harrington, L. G. Mental disorders among domiciled veterans. *Journal of the American Geriatrics Society*, 1964, *12*, 562-565.

Anonymous. Senile mental deterioration. *British Medical Journal*, 1969, *4*, 415.

Arsenian, J. Situational factors contributing to mental illness in the elderly. *Geriatrics*, 1962, *17*, 667-674.

Barre, C. & Lalanne, F. (Dominal in the neurotic and psychiatric manifestations observed in the hospitalized aged.) *Semaine Médicale Professionnelle et Medico-Sociale*, 1962, *38*, 690-693.

Barshtein, E. I. (Clinical features of the initial stages of senile dementiating processes.) *Zhurnal Neuropatologii i Psikhiatrii*, 1968, *68*, 1204-1209.

Behrends, K. & Zimmermann, R. (The psychological disorders of the aged in social fields.) *Actuelle Gerontologie*, 1972, *2*, 77-81.

Beiser, M. A psychiatric follow-up study of "normal" adults. *American Journal of Psychiatry*, 1971, *127*, 1464-1472.

Belousova, V. N., Listratenko, V. V. & Shestakova, G. I. (Clinico-statistical analysis of mental illness in later life in Amur Province.) In V. M. Banshchikov (Ed.), *Trudy Pervogo Vserossiiskogo S"Ezda Neuropatologov I Psikhiatrov*, 473-477.

Beresford, C. C. Senile dementia. *Nursing Times*, 1962, *58*, 861-864.

Bergmann, K. The epidemiology of senile dementia. *British Journal of Hospital Medicine*, 1969, *2*, 727-732.

Birke, E. R. (Disturbed states in depersonalized aged men.) *Münchener Medizinische Wochenschrift*, 1961, *103*, 1068-1072.

Birkett, D. P. The psychiatric differentiation of senility and arteriosclerosis. *British Journal of Psychiatry*, 1972, *120*, 321-325.

Bisio, B. (Mental pathology in the involutional age.) *Annali di Neuropsichiatria e Psicoanalisi*, 1961, *8*, 150-227.

Bleĭkher, V. M. (Speech disorders in senile dementia.) *Zhurnal Neuropatologii i Psikhiatrii*, 1966, *66*, 575-580.

Bourestom, N. C., Wolff, R. J. & Davis, H. R. Prognostic factors in elderly mental patients. *Clinical Medicine*, 1961, *8*, 1751-1754.

Bridges, P. K. Special psychiatric problems in relation to disabilities, congenital, acquired and geriatric. *Physiotherapy*, 1962, *48*, 175-178.

Bronisch, F. W. (*The four disturbances of old people.*) Stuttgart: Ferdinand Enke Verlag, 1962.

Busse, E. W. & Pfeiffer, E. Functional psychiatric disorders in old age. In E. W. Busse & E. Pfeiffer (Eds.), *Behavior and adaptation in late life*. Boston: Little, Brown, 1969, 183-235.

Butler, R. N. Psychiatric evaluation of the aged. *Geriatrics*, 1963, *18*, 220-232.

Butler, R. N. Patterns of psychological health and psychiatric illness in retirement. In F. M. Carp (Ed.), *The retirement process. Publication of the U. S. Department of Health, Education, and Welfare*, 1968, *1778*, 27-41.

Butler, R. N. Mental health care in old age: Conflicts in public policy. *Psychiatric Annals*, 1972, *2*, 28-44.

Cahn, L. A. Pathogenic factors in the mental disorders of old age. *Gerontologia Clinica*, 1962, *4* (Suppl.), 32-35.

Carp, F. M. Senility or garden-variety maladjustment? *Journal of Gerontology*, 1969, *24*, 203-204.

Chatagnon, P., Chatagnon, C., Mortier, D., Legembre, P. & Castel, J. (The persistence of the maternal "instinct" in the course of mental degradation. The "old women with dolls.") *Annales Médico-Psychologiques*, 1962, *120*, 561-566.

Ciompi, L. (Psychogenic disorders in old age.) *Zeitschrift für Psychotherapie und Medizinische Psychologie*, 1966, *16*, 201-211.

Corsellis, J. A. N. The pathology of dementia. *British Journal of Hospital Medicine*, 1969, *2*, 695-703.

Coulter, O. W. New hope for older mental patients. *Aging*, 1968, *161*, 3-12.

Cross, H. E. & McKusick, V. A. The mast syndrome. A recessively inherited form of presenile dementia with motor disturbances. *Archives of Neurology*, 1967, *163*, 1-13.

Daly, R. W. & Johnson, F. A. The effects of age, education and occupation on psychiatric dispositions. *Social Science and Medicine*, 1970, *4*, 619-628.

Davidson, G. A. Psychic problems in the elderly. *American Journal of Obstetrics and Gynecology*, 1966, *95*, 350-354.

Davidson, R. Mental disease in the elderly. *Gerontologia Clinica*, 1968, *10*, 293-298.

Davies, A. D. M. Measures of mental deterioration in aging and brain damage. *Interdisciplinary Topics in Gerontology*, 1968, *1*, 78-90.

Davies, G. V. The differential diagnosis of the mental disorders of late life. *Medical Journal of Australia*, 1969, *1*, 242-245.

Demuth, E. L. (Some psychiatric problems of old men.) *Revue Lyonnaise de Médicine*, 1960, *9*, 883-885. (Abstract in *Excerpta Medica*, Sect. 20, 1961, *4*, 1251.)

Dettmering, P. (A side activity.) *Praxis der Psychotherapie*, 1970, *15*, 249-252.

Doil'nitsyna, A. D. & Zubarev, Y. G. (Rheoencephalographic and electro-encephalographic comparisons in elderly mental patients.) *Zhurnal Neuropatologii i Psikhiatrii*, 1969, *69*, 1214-1218.

Drietomszky, E. Psychiatric examination. In L. Haranghy (Ed.), *Gerontological studies on Hungarian centenarians*. Budapest: Akadémiai Kiadó, 1965, 77-105.

van Dusen, W. Capacities of the aged chronic mentally ill. *California Mental Health Research Digest*, 1968, *6*, 136-137. (Abstract in *Excerpta Medica*, Sect. 20, 1969, *12*, 580.)

Dziduskzo, T. (On the systematic and nosologic aspects of mental disorders in advanced age.) *Neurologia i Neurochirurgia Polska*, 1962, *12*, 551-555.

Dziduskzo, T. (Epidemiology of psychiatric diseases in advanced age in the Warsaw region and its surroundings.) *Neurologia i Neurochirurgia Polska*, 1964, *14*, 655-662.

Eitner, S. & Gorn, A. M. (Gerontopsychological hygiene problems.) *Zeitschrift für Alternsforschung*, 1969, *22*, 49-54.

Embiricos, L. & Porot, D. Démence sénile. *Revue Francaise de Gérontologie*, 1971, *17*, 21-24.

Epstein, L. J., & Simon, A. Social, psychological, and physical factors in mental health and illness in old age. *Proceedings of the 7th International Congress of Gerontology.* Vienna: Wiener Medizinischen Akademie, 1966, *6*, 73-76.

Epstein, L. J. & Simon, A. Prediction of outcome of geriatric mental illness. *Interdisciplinary Topics in Gerontology,* 1969, *3*, 51-75.

Farroni, A. & Pedretti, A. Sulla malattia de menziale senile. *Giornale di Gerontologia,* 1967, *15*, 401-409.

Faruque, M. M. Mental problem in aged person. *Pakistan Journal of Geriatrics,* 1967, *5*, 6.

Fedotov, D. D. & Kopshitser, I. Z. (Problems of mental pathological structure in later life and therapeutic-prophylactic measure.) In V. M. Banshchikov (Ed.), *Trudy Pervogo Vserossiiskogo S"Ezda Neuropatologov i Psikhiatrov,* 60-67.

Fisher, J. & Pierce, R. C. A typology of mental disorders in the aged. *Journal of Gerontology,* 1967, *22*, 478-484.

Fiske, M. Some social dimensions of psychiatric disorders in old age. In C. Tibbitts & W. Donahue (Eds.), *Social and psychological aspects of aging: Aging around the world.* New York: Columbia University Press, 1962, 53-54. (*Sociological Abstracts,* 1965, *13*, B8148.)

Flügel, F. (Geriatric problems in neuropsychiatry.) *Therapiewoche,* 1969, *19*, 2044-2047.

Gaillard, J. M. (The disintegration of the body schema in elderly patients with states of dementia.) *Journal de Psychologie Normale et Pathologique,* 1970, *4*, 443-472.

Goldfarb, A. I. Psychiatric disorders of the aged; symptomatology, diagnosis and treatment. *Journal of the American Geriatrics Society,* 1960, *8*, 698-707.

Gooddy, W. Introduction to the problems of dementia. *Proceedings of the Australian Association of Neurologists,* 1969, *6*, 9-11.

Grauer, H. & Straker, M. Psychiatric evaluation of a chronically ill geriatric hospital population. *Journal of the American Geriatrics Society,* 1961, *9*, 1073-1077.

Graux, P. Démence et troubles du comportement chez les personnel âgées. *Revue Francaise de Gérontologie,* 1969, *15,* 349-352.

Greger, J. The developmental tendency and prognosis in psychiatric disorders of the elderly. *Psychiatria Clinica,* 1971, *4,* 281-307.

Grigorievskikh, V. S. (Comparative frequency of different psychopathological syndromes in young and old age.) *Zhurnal Neuropatologii i Psikhiatrii,* 1969, *69,* 396-402. (Abstract in *Excerpta Medica,* Sect. 20, 1969, *12,* 1698.)

Hacker, S. L. & Gaitz, C. M. The moral career of the elderly mental patient. *Gerontologist,* 1969, *9,* 120-127.

Hamilton, J. A. Psychiatric aspects. In E. V. Cowdry (Ed.), *The care of the geriatric patient.* (3rd ed.) St. Louis: C. V. Mosby, 1968, 113-129.

Harenko, A. (Neuropsychiatric problems of the aged.) *Duodecim,* 1967, *83,* 388-400.

van Hellemondt, G. (Dementia, an old fashioned diagnosis.) *Nederlands Tijdschrift voor Gerontologie,* 1972, *3,* 258-272.

Hesterly, S. O. Deviant response patterns as a function of chronological age. *Journal of Consulting Psychology,* 1963, *27,* 210-214.

Hirose, S. (Mental disturbances of the aged and psychiatric surgery.) *Ronen-byo,* 1963, *7,* 705-709.

van der Horst, L. Psychiatric deviations in older people. In P. From Hansen (Ed.), *Age with a future.* Copenhagen: Munksgaard, 1964, 67-73.

Howell, T. H. Pathological problems in nonagenarians. *Journal of the American Geriatrics Society,* 1964, *12,* 410-414.

Hulička, I. M. Psychologic problems of geriatric patients. *Journal of the American Geriatrics Society,* 1961, *9,* 797-803.

Ichimaru, S., Nishimura, T., Hariguchi, S., et al. (Dementia.) *Japanese Journal of Clinical Medicine,* 1969, *27,* 2214-2219.

Ivanova, T. I. (The structure of neuropsychic illnesses of people in later life according to the data of the outpatient psychoneurological center.) In V. M. Banshchikov (Ed.), *Trudy Pervogo Vserossiiskogo S"Ezda Neuropatologov i Psikhiatrov*, 466-472.

Janzarik, W. Diagnostic and nosological aspects of mental disorder in old age. In R. H. Williams, C. Tibbitts & W. Donahue (Eds.), *Processes of aging. Volume I.* New York: Atherton Press, 1963, 383-401.

Jones, L. H. *Senility; is it synonymous with age?* Bensenville, Ill.: Bensenville Home Society, 1971.

Jonsson, C. O., Waldton, S. & Mälhammar, G. The psychiatric symptomatology in senile dementia assessed by means of an interview. *Acta Psychiatrica Scandinavica*, 1972, *48*, 103-121.

Kaneko, J. (The actual status of senile dementia and its environment.) *Japanese Journal of Geriatrics*, 1964, *1* (Suppl.), 103-105.

Kaneko, J. (Aging and the brain from the psychiatric point of view.) *Advanced Neurological Science*, 1967, *11*, 644-648.

Kaneko, J. & Tachibana, K. (Medical and sociological problem in geriatric psychiatric patients.) *Japanese Journal of Geriatrics*, 1970, 7, 219-229.

Kassel, V. Senility — A definition. *Rocky Mountain Medical Journal*, 1965, *62*, 51-52.

Kastenbaum, R. Multiple personality in later life — A developmental interpretation. *Gerontologist*, 1964, *4*, 16-19.

Kaufman, M. R. Functional and organic mental disorders in the elderly. *Journal of Mount Sinai Hospital*, 1965, *32*, 615-621.

Kay, D. W. K., Beamish, P. & Roth, M. R. Old age mental disorders in Newcastle-upon-Tyne. Part I. A study of prevalence. Part II. A study of possible social and medical causes. *British Journal of Psychiatry*, 1964, *110*, 146-158; 668-682. (Abstract in *Excerpta Medica*, Sect. 20, 1965, *8*, 1218-1219.)

Kidd, C. B. The changing outcome of mental illness in old age. *Ulster Medical Journal*, 1962, *31*, 88-92.

Kidd, C. B. & Kingham, J. An anthropological study of the elderly patient in an adult psychiatric clinic. *International Journal of Social Psychiatry*, 1967, *13*, 115-125.

Kidd, C. The operational value of epidemiological data in geriatric psychiatry. *Australian and New Zealand Journal of Psychiatry*, 1969, *3*, 58-60.

Kiloh, L. G. Pseudo-dementia. *Acta Psychiatrica Scandinavica*, 1961, *37*, 336-351.

Komatsubara, T. (Three types of dementia senilis.) *Ronen-byo*, 1964, *8*, 174-177.

Kopits, I. Observations on 750 geropsychiatric patients. *Journal of the American Geriatrics Society*, 1970, *18*, 353-364.

Kral, V. A. Stress and mental disorders of the senium. *Medical Service Journal*, 1962, *18*, 363-370.

Kral, V. A. Senile dementia and normal aging. *Journal of the Canadian Psychiatric Association*, 1972, *17* (Suppl. 2), SS25.

Kral, V. A. Psychiatric problems in the aged; a reconsideration. *Journal of the Canadian Psychiatric Association*, 1973, *108*, 584.

Kraus, J. Relationship of psychiatric diagnoses, hospital admission rates, and size and age structure of immigrant groups. *Medical Journal of Australia*, 1969, *2*, 91.

Kühne, G. E. (Sociopsychiatric aspects of aged patients.) *Zeitschrift für Ärztliche Fortbildung*, 1967, *61*, 976-979.

Kvadsheim, H. (Mental disease in the aged (geronto-psychiatry).) *Tidsskrift for den Norske Laegeforening*, 1965, *86*, 1647-1648.

Lambo, T. A. Psychiatric disorders in the aged; epidemiology and preventive measures. *West African Medical Journal*, 1966, *15*, 121-124.

Larsson, T., Sjögren, T., & Jacobsen, G. Senile dementia; a clinical, sociomedical and genetic study. *Acta Psychiatrica Scandinavica*, 1963, *39* (Suppl. 167), 1-259.

Larsson, T. Aetiology and epidemiology of senile dementia. In P. From Hansen (Ed.), *Age with a future.* Copenhagen: Munksgaard, 1964, 648-654.

Lelièvre-Lalligier, A. (Dementia, psychopathies and behavior disorders in the aged.) *Lille Médical,* 1969, *14,* 719-722.

Linden, M. E. Older people and mental impairment. *Rehabilitation Record,* 1966, *7,* 28-32.

Lissitz, S. The challenge of the senile aged. *Gerontologist,* 1969, *9,* 114-119.

Lopez Ibor, J. J. Alteraciones psiquiátricas en el anciano. *Revista Española de Gerontologia,* 1967, *2,* 315-329.

Lowenthal, M. F. Some social dimensions of psychiatric disorders in old age. In R. H. Williams, C. Tibbitts & W. Donahue (Eds.), *Processes of aging. Volume II.* New York: Atherton Press, 1963, 224-246.

Lowenthal, M. F. Social isolation and mental illness in old age. In P. From Hansen (Ed.), *Age with a future.* Copenhagen: Munksgaard, 1964, 463-470.

Lowenthal, M. F. & Berkman, P. L. The problem of rating psychiatric disability in a study of normal and abnormal aging. *Journal of Health and Human Behavior,* 1964, *5,* 40-44. (*Sociological Abstracts,* 1964, *12,* 1441.)

Lowenthal, M. F. *Lives in distress; the paths of the elderly to the psychiatric ward.* New York: Basic Books, 1964. (*Psychological Abstracts,* 1965, *39,* 2262.)

Lowenthal, M. F., Berkman, P. L., Brissette, G. G., Buehler, J. A., Pierce, R. C., Robinson, B. C. & Trier, M. L. *Aging and mental disorder in San Francisco.* San Francisco: Jossey-Bass, 1967.

Lowenthal, M. F. Social isolation and mental illness in old age. In B. L. Neugarten (Ed.), *Middle age and aging.* Chicago: University of Chicago Press, 1968, 220-234.

Macmillan, D. & Shaw, P. Senile breakdown in standards of personal and environmental cleanliness. *British Medical Journal,* 1966, *2,* 1032-1037.

Macmillan, D. Features of senile breakdown. *Geriatrics*, 1969, *24*, 109-118.

Manson, M. P. Study of a geriatric psychiatric population. *Geriatrics*, 1961, *16*, 612-618.

Marchand, L. (Anatomo-clinico-genetic considerations on mental disorders in aged persons.) *Annales Médico-Psychologiques*, 1963, *2*, 161-179.

Mario Strejilevich, S. (Psychological aspects and psychiatry of the aged. Medical Rx in psychiatric gerontology.) *Revista Española de Gerontologia*, 1971, *6*, 195-204.

Marks, I. M. & Gelder, M. G. Different ages of onset in varieties of phobia. *American Journal of Psychiatry*, 1966, *123*, 218-221.

Maruyama, Y., Kishimoti, A., Sekiyama, A. & Mochizuki, A. (Mental disturbance of the aged (pilot study).) *Bulletin of the Seishin-igaku Institute*, 1964, *11*, 1-8.

Maruyama, Y., Kishimoti, A., Sekiyama, A. & Mochizuki, A. (Mental disturbance of the aged (pilot study).) *Acta Gerontologica Japonica* (Yokufuen Chosa Kenkyu Kiyo), 1965, *42*, 1-8. (English Abstract, p. 1.)

Maryland. Department of Mental Hygiene. Statistics Section. *Mental health and mental illness in Maryland.* Baltimore: State Printers, 1969.

Matsuda, T., Shinohara, S. & Suzuki, T. Study of the prognosis of presenile and senile neuropsychiatric diseases. *Ronen-byo*, 1963, *7*, 615-621.

McDonald, C. Clinical heterogeneity in senile dementia. *British Journal of Psychiatry*, 1969, *115*, 267-271.

Mensh, I. N. Studies of older psychiatric patients. *Gerontologist*, 1963, *3*, 100-104.

Meyer, H. H. (Mental diseases in old age.) *Deutsches Medizinisches Journal*, 1961, *12*, 396-400.

Meyer, H. H. (Behavior disturbances and mental diseases of the aging man.) *Hippokrates,* 1967, *38,* 352-357.

Morris, P. A. A survey of 100 female senile admissions to a mental hospital. *Journal of Mental Science,* 1962, *108,* 801-803.

Müller, C. (The influence of age on preexisting mental disease.) *Schweizerische Medizinische Wochenschrift,* 1965, *95,* 1001-1005.

Müller, C. & Ciompi, L. *Senile dementia.* Bern: Hans Huber, 1968.

Müller, H. F. & Kral, V. A. The electroencephalogram in advanced senile dementia. *Journal of the American Geriatrics Society,* 1967, *15,* 415-426.

Munch-Petersen, S. Problems relating to patients with senile dementia. *Acta Psychiatrica Scandinavica,* 1966, *42* (Suppl. 191), 99.

Nielsen, J. (Geriatric psychiatric problems in a limited population group.) *Ugeskrift for Laeger,* 1962, *124,* 1652-1656.

Nielsen, J. Geronto-psychiatric period-prevalence investigation in a geographically delimited population. *Acta Psychiatrica Scandinavica,* 1962, *38,* 307-330.

Nielsen, J. Geriatric-psychiatric investigation within a geographically delineated population group. *Acta Psychiatrica Scandinavica,* 1963, *39* (Suppl. 169), 203-205. (Abstract in *Excerpta Medica,* Sect. 20, 1965, *8,* 1222.)

Noy, P. (Psychiatric problems in old age.) *Harefuah,* 1963, *65,* 51-54.

Oakley, D. P. Senile dementia; some aetiological factors. *British Journal of Psychiatry,* 1965, *111,* 414-419. (*Psychological Abstracts,* 1965, *39,* 12044.)

de Onzono, I., Garzon, C.,& Boya, J. (Comparative study of involutive cerebral disturbances in mental patients.) *Archivos de Neurobiologia,* 1970, *33,* 431-451.

Pasamanick, B. A survey of mental disease in a urban population. VI. An approach to total prevalence by age. *Mental Hygiene,* 1962, *46,* 567-572.

Perlin, S. & Butler, R. N. Psychiatric aspects of adaptation to the aging experience. In J. E. Birren, R. N. Butler, S. W. Greenhouse, L. Sokoloff, & M. R. Yarrow (Eds.), *Human aging. Publication of the U. S. Public Health Service*, 1963, *986*, 159-216.

Perron, R. (Aging and mental deterioration; a method of study and some results.) *Colloques Internaux de Centre National de la Recherche Scientifique. Le Vieillissement de Fonctions Psychologiques et Psychophysiologiques.* Paris: Centre National de la Recherche Scientifique, 1961, 107-117.

Pichot, P. & Lajeunesse, S. (Problems posed by the ncsography in senile dementia.) *Problèmes en gériatrie.* Paris: Sandoz Éditions, 1968, 233-248.

Pirozynski, T., Tomorug, E., & Scripcaru, G. (Observations of the antisocial behavior of aged persons with mental disorders.) *Annales Médico-Psychologiques*, 1968, *1*, 231-237.

Pokorny, A. D. & Overall, J. E. Relationships of psychopathology to age, sex, ethnicity, education and marital status in state hospital patients. *Journal of Psychiatric Research*, 1970, *7*, 143-152.

Poppe, W. & Lange, E. (On the prognosis of mental cerebral decompensation state in old age.) *Deutsche Gesundheitswesen*, 1964, *19*, 640-645.

Post, F. Somatic and psychic factors in the treatment of elderly psychiatric patients. *Journal of Psychosomatic Research*, 1966, *10*, 13-18.

Postel, J., Rancoule, M., Postel, M. & Luksemberg, M. (Prevention of psychic defects in the aged.) *Annales Médico-Psychologiques*, 1961, *119*, 833-848.

Postel, J., Rancoule, M., Postel, M. & Luksemberg, M. (Psychic failure of the aged.) *Annales Médico-Psychologiques*, 1961, *119*, 877-912.

Postel, J. & Postel, M. (Mental decay of the aged person and its prevention.) *Gazette Médicale de France*, 1962, *69*, 1687-1696.

Postel, J. (Difficulty of recognizing oneself in the mirror in late dementia.) *Evolution Psychiatrique*, 1968, *33*, 605-648.

Predescu, V., Roman, I., Ionescu, G., et al. (Unusual somatic and mental aspects of affective syndromes and psychoses in advanced age.) *Neurologia,* (Bucurest), 1967, *12,* 253-263.

Predescu, V., Pirée, S., & Damian, N. (Psychogenic factors in psychiatric pathology in the aged.) *Neurologia,* (Bucurest), 1968, *13,* 97-107.

Raskin, N. H. Dementia. *California Medicine,* 1969, *111,* 227-228.

Reimann, H. & Hafner, H. Mental disorders of the elderly in Mannheim: An investigation of incidence rate. *Social Psychiatry,* 1972, *7,* 53-69.

de Risio, C., Urbani, M., & Ridolo, P. (The orienting reflex in senile dementia.) *Revista di Neurobiologia,* 1966, *12,* 589-595.

Robinson, R. A. The diagnosis and prognosis of dementia. In W. F. Anderson & B. Isaacs (Eds.), *Current achievements in geriatrics.* London: Cassell, 1964, 190-203.

Rose, A. The prevalence of mental disorders in Italy. *International Journal of Social Psychiatry,* 1964, *10,* 87-100. (*Psychological Abstracts,* 1967, *41,* 1631.)

Rosenblum, M. P. & Bachrach, D. L. Study of behavioral aspects of the aging psychiatric patient. *Geriatrics,* 1963, *18,* 247-250.

Roth, M. & Kay, D. W. K. Social, medical and personality factors associated with vulnerability to psychiatric breakdown in old age. *Gerontologia Clinica,* 1962, *4,* 147-160.

Roth, M. Cerebral disease and mental disorders of old age as causes of antisocial behavior. *International Psychiatric Clinic,* 1968, *5,* 35-58.

Roth, M. Mental health problems of ageing and the aged with some comments on the role of world health and other international organizations. *Work and aging,* 2nd, International Course in Social Gerontology. Paris: International Center of Social Gerontology, 1971, 83-107.

Rouart, J. (The ages of life and psychopathology.) *Evolution Psychiatrique,* 1963, *28,* 65-97.

Routsonis, C. G. (Hemianoptic hallucinations among the aged and the Charles Bonnet syndrome.) *Annales Médico-Psychologiques*, 1969, *2*, 309-316.

Rubino, A. Psicopatologia dell'anziano. *Giornale di Gerontologia*, 1972, *20*, 919-934.

Rubinshtein, S. Y. (A study of the breakdown of habits in the elderly mentally ill.) In B. V. Zelgarnik (Ed.), *Voprosy E-Ksperimental'noi Patopsikhologii*, Moscow, 1965, 58-67. (Gosudarstuennyi Nauchno-Issledovatel'skii Institut Psikhiatrii. Trudy, t. 43.)

Rudd, T. N. Mental aberrations of old age. *Medical World*, 1968, *106*, 20-24.

Salmon, J. H. Senile and presenile dementia. *Geriatrics*, 1969, *24*, 67-72.

Sanderson, R. E. & Inglis, J. Learning and mortality in elderly psychiatric patients. *Journal of Gerontology*, 1961, *16*, 375-376.

Schaumburg, H. H. & Suzuki, K. Nonspecific familial presenile dementia. *Journal of Neurology, Neurosurgery, and Psychiatry*, 1968, *31*, 479-486.

Schergna, E. & Crosato, F. (Correlations between the mental deterioration and the entity of atrophy in the primary and secondary presenile and senile atrophic syndromes.) *Giornale di Psichiatria e di Neuropatologia*, 1961, *89*, 1-27.

Schindler, R. (Mental decompensation in the elderly; preventive measures.) *Schweizerische Medizinische Wochenschrift*, 1965, *95*, 995-1001. (*Psychological Abstracts*, 1965, *39*, 14798.)

Shternberg, E. I. (Interrelations between the psychology and the psychopathology of old age.) *Zhurnal Neuropatologii i Psikhiatrii*, 1971, *71*, 835-840.

Shulman, R. A survey of vitamin B_{12} deficiency in an elderly psychiatric population. *British Journal of Psychiatry*, 1967, *113*, 241-251.

Simon, A. & Neal, M. W. Patterns of geriatric mental illness. In R. H. Williams, C. Tibbitts & W. Donahue (Eds.), *Processes of aging. Volume I.* New York: Atherton Press, 1963, 449-471.

Simon, A. The geriatric mentally ill. *Gerontologist,* 1968, *8,* 7-15.

Simon, A. Physical and socio-psychologic stress in the geriatric mentally ill. *Comprehensive Psychiatry,* 1970, *11,* 242-247.

Simon, A. The psychiatrist and the geriatric patient. Screening of the aged mentally ill. *Journal of Geriatric Psychiatry,* 1970, *4,* 5-17.

Sinha, S. N. Socio psychological aspects of mental illness in the aged. *Indian Journal of Gerontology,* 1971, *3,* 36-38.

Sloane, R. B. & Frank, D. The mentally afflicted old person. *Geriatrics,* 1970, *25,* 125-132.

Stangle, E. K. Geriatric psychiatry and social gerontology. *Journal of the American Geriatrics Society,* 1969, *17,* 612-618.

Stoerger, R. (Mental disorders in old age including therapeutic view-points.) *Medizinische Monatsschrift,* 1968, *22,* 393-397.

Stotsky, B. A. & Rhetts, J. E. Factorial study of psychopathology in psychiatric patients successfully placed in nursing homes. *Journal of the American Geriatrics Society,* 1967, *15,* 437-447.

Straker, M. Prognosis for psychiatric illness in the aged. *American Journal of Psychiatry,* 1963, *119,* 1069-1075.

Strömgren, E. Epidemiology of old-age psychiatric disorders. In R. H. Williams, C. Tibbitts & W. Donahue (Eds.), *Processes of aging. Volume II.* New York: Atherton Press, 1963, 133-151.

Strömgren, E. Psychiatric deviations in older people. In P. From Hansen (Ed.), *Age with a future.* Copenhagen: Munksgaard, 1964, 74-75.

Strömgren, E. Recent studies on prevalence of mental disorders in the aged. In P. From Hansen (Ed.), *Age with a future.* Copenhagen: Munksgaard, 1964, 243-247.

Szewczyk, H. (Psychiatric and neurological point of view in the elderly.) In G. Brüschke & F. H. Schulz (Eds.), *Fibel für die praktische Geriatrie.* Jena: VEB Gustav Fischer Verlag, 1969, 292-303.

Tramer, L. & Bentovim, L. Reactive behavioral disorders of aged. *Psychiatria et Neurologia*, 1961, *142*, 376-386.

Trier, T. R. Characteristics of mentally ill aged; a comparison of patients with psychogenic disorders and patients with organic brain syndromes. *Journal of Gerontology*, 1966, *21*, 354-364.

Tripi, E. (Gero-psychiatric problem. Review; biological, psychological and pathological aspects of old age. Statistico-clinical studies of the inmates of mental hospitals. Mental hygiene measures.) *Ospedale Psichiatrico*, 1969, *37*, 233-268. (Abstract in *Excerpta Medica*, Sect. 20, 1970, *13*, 820.)

Udelman, H. D. Geriatric psychiatry. A global view. *Arizona Medicine*, 1973, *30*, 89-91.

U. S. Department of Health, Education and Welfare. Public Health Service. *Mental disorders of the aging. Publication of the U. S. Public Health Service*, 1963, *993*, 1-19.

Various. Aging — A survey of the psychiatric literature, 1961-1964. In S. Levin & R. J. Kahana (Eds.), *Psychodynamic studies on aging; creativity, reminiscing, and dying*. New York: International Universities Press, 1967, 221-318.

Various. (Psychosocial considerations on the psychiatric old person.) *Revue d'Hygiene et de Médicine Sociale*, 1968, *16*, 583-612.

Verwoerdt, A. Clinical geropsychiatry. In A. B. Chinn (Ed.), *Working with older people; a guide to practice. Volume IV. Clinical aspects of aging. Publication of the U. S. Public Health Service*, 1971, *1459*, 60-80.

Walsh, A. C. Senile dementia. *Pennsylvania Medicine*, 1967, *70*, 55-59.

Watson, C. G. & Fulton, J. R. Treatment potential of the psychiatric-medically infirm. II. Psychiatric symptomatology. *Journal of Gerontology*, 1968, *23*, 226-230.

Weinberg, A. A. (Encroachment on mental health as the result of environmental change and loneliness and possibilities of prevention.) *Zeitschrift für Psychotherapie und Medizinische Psychologie*, 1969, *19*, 45-51.

Weiss, H. J. *Personality development and psychopathology in the later years.* Cleveland: Training Institute for Public Welfare Personnel in Aging, 1965.

Weiss, J. M. A., Willis, B. B., Jones, J. M., Schaie, K. W., Robins, A. J. & Fields, G. L. Predicting the psychiatric problems of older persons; a follow-up study. In C. Tibbitts & W. Donahue (Eds.), *Social and psychological aspects of aging.* New York: Columbia University Press, 1962, 568-577.

Weiss, J. M. A. & Schaie, K. W. Symptom formation among older patients in a psychiatric clinic population. In H. T. Blumenthal (Ed.), *Medical and clinical aspects of aging.* New York: Columbia University Press, 1962, 64-71.

Wolff, K. The disturbed geriatric patient. *Journal of the American Geriatrics Society*, 1965, *12*, 1134-1137.

Wolff, K. The elder patient. Psychiatric disorders and their management. *Journal of the American Geriatrics Society*, 1967, *15*, 575-586.

Yasunaga, H. (Aged people and mental disorders.) *Ronen-byo*, 1961, *5*, 523-534.

Young, J. P. Acute psychiatric disturbances in the elderly and their treatment. *British Journal of Clinical Practice*, 1972, *26*, 513-516.

Zamykal, A. (Analysis of gerontopsychiatric cases.) *Československa Psychiatrie*, 1962, *58*, 95-97.

III. GENERAL GERIATRIC PSYCHIATRY

Anonymous. (Geriatric psychiatry.) *Psychiatria et Neurologia Japonica,* 1967, *69,* 1060-1085.

Averbuch, E. S. (Psychiatric aspect of gerontology and geriatrics.) In N. N. Gorev (Ed.), *(Problems of gerontology and geriatrics.)* Kiev: State Publishing House of Medical Literature, 1962, 108+.

Balier, C. L'intervention du psychiatre en gérontologie. *Revue Francaise de Gérontologie,* 1966, *12,* 165-168.

Bergener, M., Hummel, F.,& Reinhart, H. Vordringliche Probleme und Aufgaben der Gerontopsychiatrie. *Veröffentlichungen der Deutschen Gesellschaft für Gerontologie,* 1970, *4,* 294-301.

Biernacki, T. & Sulestrowski, W. (Geriatrics in psychiatry.) *Wiadomości Lekarskie,* 1968, *21,* 2173-2177. (Abstract in *Excerpta Medica,* Sect. 20, 1969, *12,* 1084.)

Borghesi, R. & Medaglini, E. (Aspects of geronto-psychiatry. (Statistical study).) *Rassegna di Studi Psichiatrici,* 1963, *52,* 443-451.

Butler, R. N. Clinical psychiatry in late life. In I. Rossman (Ed.), *Clinical geriatrics.* Philadelphia: J. B. Lippincott, 1971, 439-459.

Butler, R. N. The responsibility of psychiatry to the elderly. *American Journal of Psychiatry,* 1971, *127,* 1080-1081.

Carter, J. H. Psychiatry, racism and aging. *Journal of the American Geriatrics Society,* 1972, *20,* 343-346.

Dedieu-Anglade, G. (Psychiatric gerontology.) *Revue Francaise de Gérontologie,* 1962, *8,* 383-385.

Shternberg, E. Y. (Gerontopsychiatry.) *Zhurnal Neuropatologii i Psikhiatrii,* 1967, *67,* 1733-1739.

Shternberg, E. Y. (The psychology of aging and old age and its significance for gerontopsychiatry.) *Zhurnal Neuropatologii i Psikhiatrii,* 1968, *68,* 1238-1251.

Simon, A. & Esser, M. A. Review of psychiatric progress 1964. Geriatrics. *American Journal of Psychiatry,* 1965, *121,* 682-685.

Smith, J. A. Geriatric psychiatry. *Psychosomatics,* 1967, *8,* 56-58.

Stenbäck, A. Research in geriatric psychiatry and the care of the aged. *Comprehensive Psychiatry,* 1973, *14,* 9-15.

Stotsky, B. A. Social and clinical issues in geriatric psychiatry. *American Journal of Psychiatry,* 1972, *129,* 117-126.

Verwoerdt, A. & Eisdorfer, C. Geropsychiatry: The psychiatry of senescence. *Geriatrics,* 1967, *22,* 139-149.

Verwoerdt, A. Psychiatric aspects of aging. In R. R. Boyd & C. G. Oakes (Eds.), *Foundations of practical gerontology.* Columbia: University of South Carolina Press, 1969, 117-139.

Wolff, K. *Geriatric psychiatry.* Springfield, III.: Charles C. Thomas, 1963.

Zimberg, S. The psychiatrist and medical home care; geriatric psychiatry in the Harlem community. *American Journal of Psychiatry,* 1971, *127,* 1062-1066.

Zinberg, N. E. Geriatric psychiatry; need and problems. *Gerontologist,* 1964, *4,* 130-135.

IV. ORGANIC BRAIN SYNDROME

A. Chronic Brain Syndrome

de Ajuriaguerra, J., Rego, A., & Tissot, R. (Stereotyped motor activities in dementias.) *Annales Médico-Psychologiques,* 1963, *121,* 641-664.

de Ajuriaguerra, J., Boehme, M., Richard, J., et al. (Disintegration of the elements of time in the degenerative dementias of old age.) *Encephale,* 1967, *56,* 385-438.

Bergener, M. (The concept of dementia — Organic brain syndrome or psychopathological dogma.) *Verhandlungen der Deutschen Gesellschaft für Innere Medizin,* 1969, *75,* 1003-1006.

Dorfman, W. Is there a "reversible" chronic brain syndrome? *Psychosomatics,* 1967, *8,* 293-295.

Elam, L. H. & Blumenthal, H. T. Aging in the mentally retarded. *Interdisciplinary Topics in Gerontology,* 1970, *7,* 87-117.

Fisch, M., Goldfarb, A. I.,& Shahinian, S. P. Chronic brain syndrome in the community aged. *Archives of General Psychiatry,* 1968, *18,* 739-745.

Foley, J. M. Differential diagnosis of the organic mental disorders in elderly patients. *Advances in Behavioral Biology,* 1972, *3,* 153-161.

Harris, R. The relationship between organic brain disease and physical status. *Advances in Behavioral Biology,* 1972, *3,* 163-177.

Hillman, W. A., Jr. & Libro, A. C. Aging in retardation. *Journal of Psychiatric Nursing,* 1966, *4,* 540-545.

Anonymous. Measures of dementia and senile change. *Lancet,* 1969, *1,* 88-89.

Bettner, L. G., Jarvik, L. F., & Blum, J. E. Stroop Color-Word Test, non-psychotic organic brain syndrome, and chromosome loss in aged twins. *Journal of Gerontology,* 1971, *26,* 458-469.

Bettner, L. G. & Blum, J. E. Kent-Rosanoff Free Association Test in aged twins with and without organic brain syndrome. *Proceedings of the American Psychological Association,* 1972, *7,* 651-652.

Borghesi, R. (Moral judgement and the Tsedek test in senile dementia.) *Rassegna di Studi Psichiatrici,* 1963, *52,* 414-420.

Bovi, A. (Cerebral rheography in the differential standards of senile psychoses and arteriosclerotic psychoses.) *Giornale di Psichiatria e di Neuropatologia,* 1961, *89,* 1527-1540.

Braceland, F. J. Psychopathology of the aging. *Postgraduate Medicine,* 1962, *32,* 278-283.

Canter, A. & Straumanis, J. J. Performance of senile and healthy aged persons on the BIP Bender Test. *Perceptual and Motor Skills,* 1969, *28,* 695-698.

Currie, J. S., Anderson, R. J., & Price, A. C. Timed block counting as a test for organic brain impairment. *Journal of Gerontology,* 1965, *20,* 372-373.

Evans, R. B. & Marmorston, J. Psychological test signs of brain damage in cerebral thrombosis. *Psychological Reports,* 1963, *12,* 915-930.

Gordon, E. B. Serial EEG studies in presenile dementia. *British Journal of Psychiatry,* 1968, *114,* 779-780.

Suchett-Kaye, A.I., Sarkar, U., Elkan, G., & Waring, M. Physical, mental and social assessment of elderly patients suffering from cerebrovascular accident with special reference to rehabilitation. *Gerontologia Clinica,* 1971, *13,* 192-206.

V. PSYCHOSES

A. General

Akesson, H. O. A population study of senile and arteriosclerotic psychoses. *Human Heredity,* 1969, *19,* 546-556. (*Psychological Abstracts,* 1971, *45,* 10350.)

Akesson, H. O. (Senile and arteriosclerotic psychosis. A population study.) *Läkartidningen,* 1969, *66,* 118-124.

Aripov, N. A. (Emotional disorders in psychoses during old age.) *Meditsinkii Zhurnal Uzbekistana,* 1963, *10,* 51-54.

Averbuch, E. S. (Particularities of personality and personal reactions of patients suffering from circulatory and involutional (presenile and senile) psychoses.) In D. F. Chebotarev (Ed.), (*Problems of gerontology and geriatrics, Volume III. Mechanisms of aging.*) Kiev: State Publishing House of Medical Literature, 1963, 262-264.

Averbuch, E. S. (Understanding the nature of non-dement forms of presenile and senile psychoses.) *Zhurnal Neuropatologii i Psikhiatrii,* 1971, *71,* 1820-1824.

Bagh, K. (Involution psychosis and presenile dementia. A review.) *Duodecim,* 1965, *81,* 374-381.

Bucci, L. Senile psychosis and paraphrenia; some theoretical and practical considerations. *International Journal of Neuropsychiatry,* 1965, *1,* 561-566.

Caird, W. K. Memory loss in the senile psychoses; organic or psychogenic? *Psychological Reports,* 1966, *18,* 788-790.

Calvo Melendro, J. (Senile psychosis.) *Anales de la Real Academia Nacional de Medicina,* 1966, *83,* 413-428.

Campailla, G. (Emotional factors in the pathogenesis of senile and arteriosclerotic psychoses.) *Nervenarzt,* 1962, *33,* 145-150.

Christozov, C. (Psychoses of the involution age (presenile psychoses).) *Maroc Médical,* 1970, *538,* 529-533.

Compoy Guerrero, A. (Psychotic disorders and dementia in the aged.) *Revista Española de Gerontología,* 1971, *6,* 169-174.

Constantinidis, J., Garrone, G., & de Ajuriaguerra, J. (The inheritance of senile psychoses.) *Encéphale,* 1962, *51,* 301-344.

Dominick, J. R. Nursing care factors in psychotic depressive reactions in elderly patients. *Perspective Psychiatric Care,* 1968, *6,* 28-32.

Ehrentheil, O. F. Behavioral changes of aging chronic psychotics. In R. Kastenbaum (Ed.), *New thoughts on old age.* New York: Springer, 1964, 99-115.

Epstein, L., Simon, A., & Mock, R. Clinical neuropathologic correlations in senile and cerebral arteriosclerotic psychoses. In P. From Hansen (Ed.), *Age with a future.* Copenhagen: Munksgaard, 1964, 272-275.

Facchetti, G. & Miglio, G. (Vitamin C and senile psychosis and confusional state.) *Annali di Neuropsichiatria e Psicoanalisi,* 1961, *8,* 269-278.

Ferm, L. & Harenko, A. (Psychological research on senile psychoses. I. The stage of the dementia and the ability to write. II. The stage of the dementia and the handiness.) *Geron* (Societas Gerontologica Fennica), 1966-1967, *18,* 36-45.

Giannelli, A. (On the incidence and importance of situational factors in involutional psychoses.) *Giornale di Gerontologia,* 1972, *20,* 955-964.

Gibson, A. C. Psychosis occurring in the senium; a review of an industrial population. *Journal of Mental Science,* 1961, *107,* 921-925.

Gruenberg, E. M. On the frequency of geriatric psychoses by age and sex. *Interdisciplinary Topics in Gerontology,* 1969, *3,* 45-49.

Ivanova, N. S. On the developmental forms of the verbal hallucinosis syndrome during psychoses of old age. *Zhurncl Neuropatologii i Psikhiatrii*, 1965, *65*, 584-592. (*Psychologicai Abstracts*, 1965, *39*, 12821.)

Jislin, S. G. (On some clinical regularities in organic psychoses of old age.) In V. V. Alpatov (Ed.), (*Problems of gerontology*.) Moscow: Publishing House of the Academy of Sciences, 1962, 195-200.

Kim, K. The etiological significance of menopause, personality and socio-cultural factors in involutional psychoses. *Nebraska State Medical Journal*, 1961, *46*, 234-239. (Abstract in *Excerpta Medica*, Sect. 20, 1962, *5*, 1422.)

Kral, V. A., Grad, B., Cramer-Azima, F., & Russell, L. Biologic, psychologic and sociologic studies in normal aged persons and patients with senile psychosis. *Journal of the American Geriatrics Society*, 1964, *12*, 21-37.

Kral, V. A. The psychopathology and neuropathology of senile and presenile psychoses. *Laval Médical*, 1967, *38*, 584-587.

Lanzkron, J. A note on age confusion in psychosis. *Psychiatric Quarterly*, 1968, *42*, 587-588.

Lenz, H. (The actual idea of aged psychoses.) *Proceedings of the 7th International Congress of Gerontology*. Vienna: Wiener Medizinischen Akademie, 1966, *3*, 21-26.

Löffler-Schnebli, M. (Pathological psychoses in the aged.) *Gerontologia Clinica*, 1962, *4* (Suppl.), 94-102.

Lukomsky, I. I. (Old age and the problem of senile psychoses.) In V. V. Alpatov (Ed.), (*Problems of gerontology*.) Moscow: Publishing House of the Academy of Sciences, 1962, 191-194.

Michelson, N. A note on age confusion in psychosis. *Psychiatric Quarterly*, 1968, *42*, 331-338.

Morozova, T. V. (Correlational analysis of ALPHA-rhythm frequency in the EEG of normal aging people and those with the psychoses of old age.) *Zhurnal Neuropatologii i Psikhiatrii*, 1970, *70*, 1667-1671.

Müller, C. The problem of the interference of senile deterioration with preexisting psychoses. *Encéphale*, 1970, *59*, 81-89.

Pakesch, E. (On the problem of the senile psychoses.) *Wiener Medizinische Wochenschrift*, 1964, *114*, 533-534.

Payne, R., Gibson, F. E., & Pittard, B. B. Social influences in senile psychosis. *Sociological Symposium*, 1969, *2*, 137-146.

Petrov, I. (The problem of involutional psychoses in the last three years.) In D. Mateeff, G. Stoinev, I. Petrov & E. Boyadzhiev (Eds.), (*Problems of gerontology and geriatrics. Volume III.*) Sofia: Medicina i Fizkultura, 1967, 147-154.

Rosso, G. (Senile psychoses.) *Annali Freniatria e Scienze Affini*, 1969, *82*, 59065.

Roth, M. & Kay, D. W. K. Psychoses among the aged. In H. T. Blumenthal (Ed.), *Medical and clinical aspects of aging*. New York: Columbia University Press, 1962, 74-96.

Sattes, H. (Aging and senile psychoses.) *Münchener Medizinische Wochenschrift*, 1961, *103*, 831-833.

Schimmelpenning, G. W. (Senile psychoses in social psychiatry.) *Medizinische Welt*, 1967, *25*, 1520+.

Schwarz, H. (Psychotic conditions in aged men.) *Zeitschrift für Ärztliche Fortbildung*, 1967, *61*, 466-469.

Semke, V. Y. (The course of psychopathic diseases in old age.) *Zhurnal Neuropatologii i Psikhiatrii*, 1964, *64*, 1688-1696. (Abstract in *Excerpta Medica*, Sect. 20, 1965, *8*, 2211.)

Shakmatov, N. F. (Clinical-statistical study of psychoses in old age.) *Zhurnal Neuropatologii i Psikhiatrii*, 1968, *68*, 220-226.

Shchedrenko, G. K. (On the nature of mental defects in presenile psychoses.) *Voprosy Psikhiatrii i Neuropatologii, Sbornik Trudov*, 1965, *11*, 270-277.

Short, M. J., Musella, L., & Wilson, W. P. Correlation of affect and EEG in senile psychoses. *Journal of Gerontology*, 1968, *23*, 324-327.

Shternberg, E. Y. (On the possibilities and criteria of nosological differentiations of the senile psychoses.) *Zhurnal Neuropatologii i Psikhiatrii*, 1968, *68*, 213-220.

Shternberg, E. Y. (Contemporary state of theory on the clinicology and classification of psychoses in later life.) In V. M. Banshchikov (Ed.), *Trudy Pervogo Vserossiiskogo S"Ezda Neuropatologov i Psikhiatrov*, 5-13.

Sternberg, E. (On several research results of the psychoses of the aged.) *Nervenarzt*, 1963, *34*, 409-412. (Abstract in *Excerpta Medica*, Sect. 20, 1964, *7*, 1910.)

Stonecypher, D. D. The cause and prevention of postoperative psychoses in the elderly. *American Journal of Ophthalmology*, 1963, *55*, 605-610.

Vispo, R. H. Pre-morbid personality in the functional psychoses of the senium. A comparison of expatients with healthy controls. *Journal of Mental Science*, 1962, *108*, 790-800.

Weinlander, M. M. Psychotics and the influence of age on SORT variables. *Journal of Clinical Psychology*, 1967, *23*, 392-393.

B. Manic-Depressive

Gregor, J., Waldmann, K. D., Klaus, M., & Ziethen, C. (Studies of the interval of phasic psychoses.) *Psychiatrie, Neurologie und Medizinische Psychologie*, 1972, *24*, 733-740.

Hopkinson, G. & Ley, P. The age of onset in manic-depressive families. *Psychiatria et Neurologia*, 1966, *152*, 217-221.

Leibovich, F. A. & Rakhlina, M. L. (Clinical and electroencephalographic studies of patients with manic-depressive psychoses in old age.) *Zhurnal Neuropatologii i Psikhiatrii*, 1967, *67*, 568-571.

Parrini, A., Barontini, F., & Petruzzi, E. Particolari aspetti psicopatologici degli stati maniacali e ipomaniacali dell'età involutiva. *Giornale di Gerontologia*, 1967, *15*, 414-416.

Paul, M. I., Cramer, H. & Bunney, W. E. Urinary adenosine 3', 5'-mono-phosphate in the switch process from depression to mania. *Science*, 1971, *171*, 300-303.

Rokhlina, M. L. Certain peculiarities of the evolution and clinical picture of manic-depressive psychosis at an advanced age. *Zhurnal Neuropatologii i Psikhiatrii*, 1965, *65*, 567-574. *Psychological Abstracts*, 1965, *39*, 12881.)

Sedivec, V. (Progressive activity of manio-melancholic psychosis during aging and senium.) *Československa Psychiatrie*, 1971, *67*, 143-150.

C. Schizophrenia

Anonymous. Schizophrenia in old age. *British Medical Journal*, 1962, *5271*, 102.

Blanc, M., Bourgeois, M., & Favarel-Garrigues, B. (Concerning a paraphrenic.) *Annales Médico-Psychologiques*, 1967, *1*, 289.

Böszörményi, Z., Kardos, G., & Srágli, G. Gerontopsychiatric studies in schizophrenics. In A. Balázs (Ed.), *Proceedings of the International Conference on Gerontology*. Budapest: Akadémiai Kiadó, 1965, 733-736.

Callison, D. A., Armstrong, H. F., Elam, L., Cannon, R. L., Paisley, C. B., & Himwich, H. E. The effects of aging on schizophrenic and mentally defective patients; visual, auditory and grip strength measurements. *Journal of Gerontology*, 1971, *26*, 137-145.

Gamna, G., Attisani, N., & Ferrio, L. (Statistico-clinical and psychopathological considerations on a group of schizophrenics having reached old age.) *Giornale di Psichiatria e di Neuropatologia*, 1962, *90*, 767-824.

Gottheil, E. & Joseph, R. J. Age, appearance, and schizophrenia. *Archives of General Psychiatry*, 1968, *19*, 232-238.

Granville-Grossman, K. L. Parental age and schizophrenia. *British Journal of Psychiatry*, 1966, *112*, 899-905.

Grattarcla, F. R. (On the subject of senile schizophrenia.) *Acta Neurologica*, 1964, *19*, 616-625.

Hader, M. A study of aged "schizophrenogenic" parents. *Diseases of the Nervous System*, 1965, *26*, 443-445.

Hare, E. H., Price, J. S., & Slater, E. T. The age-distribution of schizophrenia and neurosis; findings in a national sample. *British Journal of Psychiatry*, 1971, *119*, 445-448.

Herbert, M. E. & Jacobson, S. Late paraphrenia. *British Journal of Psychiatry*, 1967, *113*, 461-469.

Kahana, B. & Kahana, E. Age changes in impulsivity among chronic schizophrenics. *Proceedings of the 7th International Congress of Gerontology*. Vienna: Wiener Medizinischen Akademie, 1966, *3*, 83-86.

Kay, D. W. & Roth, M. Environmental and hereditary factors in the schizophrenias of old age ("late paraphrenia"), and their bearing on the general problem of causation in schizophrenia. *Journal of Mental Science*, 1961, *107*, 649-686.

Kay, D. W. K. & Roth, M. Schizophrenias of old age. In R. H. Williams, C. Tibbitts & W. Donahue (Eds.), *Processes of aging. Volume I.* New York: Atherton Press, 1963, 402-448.

Konovalov, E. M. (Dynamics of a favorably developing schizophrenia with exacerbation in old age.) *Zhurnal Neuropatologii i Psikhiatrii*, 1971, *71*, 1069-1075.

Larson, C. A. & Nyman, G. E. Age of onset in schizophrenia. *Human Heredity*, 1970, *20*, 241-247.

Lawton, M. P. Schizophrenia forty-five years later. *Journal of Genetic Psychology*, 1972, *121*, 133-143.

Leonova, I. (Some clinical and pathophysiological criteria of the delimitation of late schizophrenia and presenile psychoses.) *Zhurnal Neuropatologii i Psikhiatrii*, 1965, *65*, 1537-1540.

Leonova, I. (Some pathophysiological criteria of diagnosing late forms of schizophrenia and presenile psychoses.) *Fiziologicheskii Zhurnal S.S.S.R. Imeni I. M. Sechenova*, 1968, *14*, 391-395.

Luka, L. & Ciompi, L. (Follow-up study on the evolution into advanced age of manic psychosis.) *Schweizer Archiv für Neurologie, Neurochirurgie und Psychiatrie*, 1970, *107*, 123-153.

Molchanova, E. K. (Clinical picture of an exacerbation of slowly evolving schizophrenia at an advanced age and features of the subsequent disease course.) *Zhurnal Neuropatologii i Psikhiatrii*, 1967, *67*, 427-431.

Müller, C. The influences of age on schizophrenia. In R. H. Williams, C. Tibbitts & W. Donahue (Eds.), *Processes of aging. Volume I.* New York: Atherton Press, 1963, 504-511.

Müller, C. Schizophrenia in advanced senescence. *British Journal of Psychiatry*, 1971, *118*, 347-348.

Post, F. Schizo-affective symptomatology in late life. *British Journal of Psychiatry*, 1971, *118*, 437-445.

Shesterneva, S. B. (Features of the course of intermittent schizophrenia in late age.) *Zhurnal Neuropatologii i Psikhiatrii*, 1968, *68*, 1362-1368. (*Psychological Abstracts*, 1970, *44*, 946.)

Shternberg, E. Y. (Clinical picture of schizophrenia viewed comparatively in the aspect of aging.) *Vestnik Akademii Meditsinskikh Nauk SSSR*, 1971, *26*, 20-23.

Sugimoto, N., Yashiki, T., Miwa, T. & Hirabayashi, K. (Investigation of intellectual death in the aged and consideration of the problem of late schizophrenia.) *Folia Psychiatria et Neurologica Japonica*, 1970, *24*, 23-36.

Sutton, S. & Zubin, J. Effect of sequence on reaction time in schizophrenia. In A. T. Welford & J. E. Birren (Eds.), *Behavior, aging, and the nervous system.* Springfield, Ill.: Charles C. Thomas, 1965, 562-597.

Venables, P. H. Slowness in schizophrenia. In A. T. Welford & J. E. Birren (Eds.), *Behavior, aging, and the nervous system.* Springfield, Ill.: Charles C. Thomas, 1965, 598-612.

Volavka, J., Matoušek, M. & Roubiček, J. EEG frequency analysis in schizophrenia. An attempt to reconsider the role of age. *Acta Psychiatrica Scandinavica*, 1966, *42*, 237-245.

Zhislina, E. S. (On the clinical and psychopathological peculiarities of delusions of persecution in schizophrenia at an advanced age.) *Zhurnal Neuropatologii i Psikhiatrii*, 1966, *66*, 1682-1688.

D. Paranoia

Berner, P. (The decline of life of paranoiacs. Contribution on the problem of relations between paranoia and paraphrenia.) *Wiener Zeitschrift für Nervenheilkunde und Deren Grenzgebiete*, 1969, *27*, 115-161.

Davidson, R. The significance of paranoia. In W. F. Anderson & B. Isaacs (Eds.), *Current achievements in geriatrics*. London: Cassell, 1964, 184-189.

Funding, T. Genetics of paranoid psychoses in later life. *Acta Psychiatrica Scandinavica*, 1961, *37*, 267-282.

Funding, T. Paranoid psychoses in later life; sociology and prognosis. *Acta Psychiatrica Scandinavica*, 1963, *39* (Suppl. 169), 356.

Greger, J. & Stahl, J. (Clinical course studies in paranoid psychosis in retrograde age.) *Archiv für Psychiatrie und Nervenkrankheiten*, 1967, *209*, 186-206.

Piatnitskaia, I. N. (On certain forms of paranoid psychosis in senility.) *Zhurnal Neuropatologii i Psikhiatrii*, 1965, *65*, 600-603. (*Psychological Abstracts*, 1965, *39*, 12824.)

Post, F. *Persistent persecutory states of the elderly*. Oxford: Pergamon Press, 1966.

Semke, V. Y. (On paranoid reactions and paranoid development in elderly psychopaths.) *Zhurnal Neuropatologii i Psikhiatrii*, 1965, *65*, 593-599. (*Psychological Abstracts*, 1965, *39*, 12828.)

Shcharina, M. G. (On paranoid delusions of jealousy in the age of involution.) *Zhurnal Neuropatologii i Psikhiatrii*, 1963, *63*, 600-606.

Simkó, A. (Of the psychopathology of the paranoid psychoses of the aged.) In A. Balázs (Ed.), *Proceedings of the International Conference on Gerontology.* Budapest: Akadémiai Kiadó, 1965, 723-727.

Sternberg, E. (The question of the paranoid psychoses of old age.) *Wissenschaftliche Zeitschrift der Humboldt-Universität zu Berlin,* 1968, *17,* 35-40.

Timofeeva, A. N. & Zamokhover, S. M. (Neurophysiologic analysis of the structure of presenile deliria of persecution.) *Zhurnal Neuropatologii i Psikhiatrii,* 1968, *68,* 1196-1204.

E. Regression

Adams, M. S. Regression in old age. *Journal of the National Medical Association,* 1972, *64,* 151-153.

Anonymous. Psychology of gerontology. 3. Factors of regression in aging. *Postgraduate Medicine,* 1971, *50,* 159.

Gillespie, W. H. Some regressive phenomena in old age. *British Journal of Medicine and Psychology,* 1963, *36,* 203-209.

Kettell, M. E. Regression and perceptual organization in normal and pathological old age. *Journal of Geriatric Psychiatry,* 1970, *3,* 187-196.

Linden, M. E. Regression and recession in the psychoses of the aging. In N. E. Zinberg & I. Kaufman (Eds.), *Normal psychology of the aging process.* New York: International Universities Press, 1963, 125-142.

Zarsky, E. L. & Blau, D. The understanding and management of narcissistic regression and dependency in an elderly woman observed over an extended period of time. *Journal of Geriatric Psychiatry,* 1970, *3,* 160-176.

Zinberg, N. E. The relationship of regressive phenomena to the aging process. In N. E. Zinberg & I. Kaufman (Eds.), *Normal psychology of the aging process.* New York: International Universities Press, 1963, 143-159.

VI. NEUROSES

A. General

Bergmann, K. Some observations on the causation of neurotic disorder in old age with special reference to physical illness. *Proceedings of the 7th International Congress of Gerontology.* Vienna: Wiener Medizinischen Akademie, 1966, *8*, 623-629.

Bergmann, K. Sex differences in the neurotic reaction of the aged. *Journal of Biosocial Science,* 1970, *2* (Suppl.), 137-145.

Bolton, N. & Savage, R. D. Neuroticism and extraversion in elderly normal subjects and psychiatric patients: Some normative data. *British Journal of Psychiatry,* 1971, *118,* 473-474.

Busse, E. W. Psychoneurotic reactions and defense mechanisms in the aged. In P. H. Hoch & J. Zubin (Eds.), *Psychopathology of aging.* New York: Grune & Stratton, 1961, 274-284.

Haits, G., Tringer, L., & Komuves, G. (Neurotic syndromes in advanced age.) *Ideggyogyaszati Szemle,* 1969, *22,* 19-33.

Henker, F. O., III. Neurologic disease in elderly psychoneurotics. *Southern Medical Journal,* 1968, *61,* 1042-1044. (Abstract in *Excerpta Medica,* Sect. 20, 1969, *12,* 1052.)

Klages, W. (Age and neurosis.) *Medizinische Klinik,* 1962, *57,* 497-501.

Klages, W. Edad y neurosis. *Archivos Panameños de Psicologia,* 1965, *1,* 263-279. (*Psychological Abstracts,* 1969, *43,* 17854.)

McDonald, C. Psychoneurosis in the elderly. *Postgraduate Medicine,* 1965, *38,* 432-437. (Abstract in *Geriatrics,* 1966, *21,* 234.)

Postema, L. J. & Schell, R. E. Aging and psychopathology: Some MMPI evidence for seemingly greater neurotic behavior among older people. *Journal of Clinical Psychology*, 1967, *23*, 140-143.

Shupe, D. R. Alphabetical neurosis and longevity. *Psychological Reports*, 1968, *22*, 630.

Sjörgren, H. *Paraphrenic, melancholic and psychoneurotic states in the presenile-senile period of life.* Copenhagen: Munksgaard, 1964.

Spiegelberg, U. & Betz, B. (Neuroses in relation to aging.) *Archiv für Psychiatrie und Nervenkrankheiten*, 1969, *212*, 294-308.

Teleshevskaia, M.E. & Pogibko, N. I. (Details of the course of neuroses and reactive states in middle age.) In N. N. Gorev (Ed.), (*Problems of gerontology and geriatrics.*) Kiev: State Publishing House of Medical Literature, 1962, 137-141.

Timsit, M. & Koninckx, N. (Statistical approach to correlations between clinical data and electroencephalographic data in neuroses.) *Acta Neurologica et Psychiatrica Belgica*, 1968, *68*, 769-786.

B. Depression — Including Hysteria

Ahmed, T. Depression. *Pakistan Journal of Geriatrics*, 1969. 7, 3-5.

de Alarcon, R. (Earlier diagnosis of depressions of the aged.) *Revista de Medicina de la Universidad de Navarra*, 1968, *12*, 193-207.

Alcala Llorente, F. & Martinez Ramon, E. (Treatment of depressive states appearing in old age.) *Medicina*, 1961, *29*, 485-498.

Anderson, D. C., Cooper, A. F.,& Naylor, G. J. Vitamin D intoxication, with hypernatraemia, potassium and water depletion, and mental depression. *British Medical Journal*, 1968, *4* (5633), 744-746.

Bart, P. B. Depression in middle-aged women: Some sociocultural factors. Unpublished doctoral dissertation, University of California, Los Angeles, 1967. (*Dissertation Abstracts International*, 1967, *28*, 4752B.)

VI. NEUROSES

A. General

Bergmann, K. Some observations on the causation of neurotic disorder in old age with special reference to physical illness. *Proceedings of the 7th International Congress of Gerontology.* Vienna: Wiener Medizinischen Akademie, 1966, *8,* 623-629.

Bergmann, K. Sex differences in the neurotic reaction of the aged. *Journal of Biosocial Science,* 1970, *2* (Suppl.), 137-145.

Bolton, N. & Savage, R. D. Neuroticism and extraversion in elderly normal subjects and psychiatric patients: Some normative data. *British Journal of Psychiatry,* 1971, *118,* 473-474.

Busse, E. W. Psychoneurotic reactions and defense mechanisms in the aged. In P. H. Hoch & J. Zubin (Eds.), *Psychopathology of aging.* New York: Grune & Stratton, 1961, 274-284.

Haits, G., Tringer, L., & Komuves, G. (Neurotic syndromes in advanced age.) *Ideggyogyaszati Szemle,* 1969, *22,* 19-33.

Henker, F. O., III. Neurologic disease in elderly psychoneurotics. *Southern Medical Journal,* 1968, *61,* 1042-1044. (Abstract in *Excerpta Medica,* Sect. 20, 1969, *12,* 1052.)

Klages, W. (Age and neurosis.) *Medizinische Klinik,* 1962, *57,* 497-501.

Klages, W. Edad y neurosis. *Archivos Panameños de Psicologia,* 1965, *1,* 263-279. (*Psychological Abstracts,* 1969, *43,* 17854.)

McDonald, C. Psychoneurosis in the elderly. *Postgraduate Medicine,* 1965, *38,* 432-437. (Abstract in *Geriatrics,* 1966, *21,* 234.)

Postema, L. J. & Schell, R. E. Aging and psychopathology: Some MMPI evidence for seemingly greater neurotic behavior among older people. *Journal of Clinical Psychology*, 1967, *23*, 140-143.

Shupe, D. R. Alphabetical neurosis and longevity. *Psychological Reports*, 1968, *22*, 630.

Sjörgren, H. *Paraphrenic, melancholic and psychoneurotic states in the presenile-senile period of life.* Copenhagen: Munksgaard, 1964.

Spiegelberg, U. & Betz, B. (Neuroses in relation to aging.) *Archiv für Psychiatrie und Nervenkrankheiten*, 1969, *212*, 294-308.

Teleshevskaia, M.E. & Pogibko, N. I. (Details of the course of neuroses and reactive states in middle age.) In N. N. Gorev (Ed.), (*Problems of gerontology and geriatrics.*) Kiev: State Publishing House of Medical Literature, 1962, 137-141.

Timsit, M. & Koninckx, N. (Statistical approach to correlations between clinical data and electroencephalographic data in neuroses.) *Acta Neurologica et Psychiatrica Belgica*, 1968, *68*, 769-786.

B. Depression — Including Hysteria

Ahmed, T. Depression. *Pakistan Journal of Geriatrics*, 1969. 7, 3-5.

de Alarcon, R. (Earlier diagnosis of depressions of the aged.) *Revista de Medicina de la Universidad de Navarra*, 1968, *12*, 193-207.

Alcala Llorente, F. & Martinez Ramon, E. (Treatment of depressive states appearing in old age.) *Medicina*, 1961, *29*, 485-498.

Anderson, D. C., Cooper, A. F.,& Naylor, G. J. Vitamin D intoxication, with hypernatraemia, potassium and water depletion, and mental depression. *British Medical Journal*, 1968, *4* (5633), 744-746.

Bart, P. B. Depression in middle-aged women: Some sociocultural factors. Unpublished doctoral dissertation, University of California, Los Angeles, 1967. (*Dissertation Abstracts International*, 1967, *28*, 4752B.)

Beck, A. T. Sexuality and depression. *Medical Aspects of Human Sexuality,* 1968, *2,* 44-51.

Birkmayer, W. & Neumayer, E. (Diagnosis and treatment of depression in old age.) *Therapeutische Umschau,* 1968, *25,* 30-32.

Böcker, F. (The cyclothymic depression in the aged.) *Medizinische Welt,* 1966, *10,* 494-495.

Borgna, E. & Smirne, S. (Chronic endogenous depression.) *Rivista di Psichiatria,* 1969, *4,* 463-478.

Botwinick, J. & Thompson, L. W. Depressive affect, speed of response, and age. *Journal of Consulting Psychology,* 1967, *31,* 106.

Bourgeois, M., Hébert, A, & Maisondieu, J. (Senile pseudo-demential conclusive-curable depressions.) *Annales Médico-Psychologiques,* 1970, *128,* 751-759.

Bowers, M. B., Jr. Clinical aspects of depression in a home for the aged. *Journal of the American Geriatrics Society,* 1969, *17,* 469-476.

Butler, R. N. Depression in old age. *Medical World News,* 1971, (Spec. Issue — Geriatrics), 64-65; 71.

Cath, S. Beyond depression; the depleted state. A study in ego psychology in the age. *Journal of the Canadian Psychiatric Association,* 1966, *11* (Suppl.), 329-339.

Chesrow, E. J. & Kaplitz, S. E. Anxiety and depression in the geriatric and chronically ill patient. *Clinical Medicine,* 1965, *72,* 1281-1284.

Ciompi, L. (The aging of hysterics; catamnestic study.) *Encéphale,* 1966, *55,* 287-335. (*Psychological Abstracts,* 1966, *40,* 13344.)

Ciompi, L. Follow-up studies on the evolution of former neurotic and depressive states in old age. Clinical and psychodynamic aspects. *Journal of Geriatric Psychiatry,* 1969, *3,* 90-106.

Ciompi, L. & Lai, G. P. (*Depression in old age.*) Bern: Huber, 1969.

Clayton, P. J., Halikas, J. A. & Maurice, W. L. The depression of widowhood. *British Journal of Psychiatry,* 1972, *120,* 71-77.

Conde, V., Escriba, J. A.,& Izquierdo, J. A. (Statistical evaluation and Spanish adaptation of Zung's Self-Rating Depression Scale: I.) *Archivos de Neurobiologia,* 1970, *33,* 185-206.

Cossa, P., Darcourt, G., & Boucebci, M. (Alternating depressive crises and crises of genuine facial neuralgia.) *Annales Medico-Psychologiques,* 1966, *2,* 538.

Cox, J. R., Pearson, R. E., & Speight, C. J. Changes in sodium, potassium and body fluid spaces in depression and dementia. *Gerontologia Clinica,* 1971, *13,* 233-245.

Crisp, A. H. & Priest, R. G. Psychoneurotic profiles in middle age: A study of persons aged 40 to 65 registered with a general practitioner. *British Journal of Psychiatry,* 1971, *119,* 385-392.

Dardenne, P., Maviel, A. & Salvador, M. Considérations sur les états dépressifs séniles. Leur traitement par le Tofranil 10mg. *Revue Francaise de Gérontologie,* 1962, *8,* 433-451.

Dorfman, W. The recognition and management of depression. *Psychosomatics,* 1970, *11,* 416-419.

Dovenmuehle, R. H. & Verwoerdt, A. Physical illness and depressive symptomatology. II. Factors of length and severity of illness and frequency of hospitalization. *Journal of Gerontology,* 1963, *18,* 260-266.

Dovenmuehle, R. H., Reckless, J. B., & Newman, G. Depressive reactions in the elderly. In E. Palmore (Ed.), *Normal aging.* Durham, N. C.: Duke University Press, 1970, 90-97.

Efimenko, V. L. (On some peculiarities of depressive states in aged persons.) *Voprosy Psikhiatrii i Neuropatologii, Sbornik Trudov,* 1966, *12,* 445-456.

Ellis, G. G., Coppen, A. & Glen, A. I. Urine concentration in depressive illness. *Journal of Neurology, Neurosurgery, and Psychiatry,* 1971, *34,* 30-31.

Farber, I. J. Age and depression. *American Journal of Psychiatry,* 1970, *126,* 1512.

Flynn, G. E. The development of the psychoanalytic concept of depression. *Journal of Psychiatric Nursing and Mental Health Services,* 1968, *6,* 138-149.

Fowlie, H. C., Cohen, C., & Anand, M. P. Depression in elderly patients with subnutrition. *Gerontologia Clinica,* 1963, *5,* 215-225.

Gabrynowicz, J. W. Depression in late life. *Medical Journal of Australia,* 1968, *1,* 299-303.

Garelli, F. F. & Fiume, S. (Demential aspects of a depressive state during senility.) *Rivista di Psichiatria,* 1966, *1,* 45-51.

Garside, R. F., et al. Depressive syndromes and the classification of patients. *Psychological Medicine,* 1971, *1,* 333-338.

Goldfarb, A. I. Masked depression in the old. *American Journal of Psychotherapy,* 1967, *21,* 791-796.

Gordon, S. K. The phenomenon of depression in old age. *Gerontologist,* 1973, *13,* 100-105.

Grauer, H. Psychodynamics of depression as seen in a geriatric out-patient clinic. *Journal of the Canadian Psychiatric Association,* 1966, *11* (Suppl.), 324-328.

Greenberg, H. R. Depressive equivalents in the pre-retirement years; "the old soldier syndrome." *Military Medicine,* 1965, *130,* 251-255.

Hader, M. Organic brain disease and depressive reactions of later life. *Journal of the Canadian Psychiatric Association,* 1966, *11* (Suppl.), 317-323.

Inglis, J. Electrode placement and the effect of E.C.T. on mood and memory in depression. *Journal of the Canadian Psychiatric Association,* 1969, *14,* 463-471.

Israel, L. & Gurfein, L. (The aging hysteric.) *Evolution Psychiatrique,* 1970, *35,* 365-376.

Kishima, C. (Clinico-genetic study of mental disorders in the aged with special reference to involutional depression.) *Bulletin of the Osaka Medical School,* 1967, *12* (Suppl.), 276.

Köknel, Ö. & Polvan, Ö. Aetiological considerations on the depressive syndromes appearing in the second half of life. *Proceedings of the 7th International Congress of Gerontology.* Vienna: Wiener Medizinischen Akademie, 1966, *3,* 47-50.

Kris, E. B. Depressions in the aged patient. *Journal of the Canadian Psychiatric Association,* 1966, *11* (Suppl.), 313-316.

Lai, G. (Psychodynamic development of depressed patients in senescence.) *Evolution Psychiatrique,* 1968, *33,* 113-137.

Leonhard, K. & Briewig, E. M. (Etiological differentiation of depressions in patients over 60 years of age.) *Archiv für Psychiatrie und Nervenkrankheiten,* 1964, *205,* 358-374.

Lesse, S. Masked depression: A diagnostic and therapeutic problem. *Diseases of the Nervous System,* 1968, *29,* 169-173.

Lesse, S. & Mathers, J. Depression sine depression: Masked depression. *New York State Journal of Medicine,* 1968, *68,* 535-543.

Levin, S. Depression in the aged; a study of the salient external factors. *Geriatrics,* 1963, *18,* 302-307.

Levin, S. Depression in the aged; the importance of external factors. In R. Kastenbaum (Ed.), *New thoughts on old age.* New York: Springer, 1964, 179-185.

Lieberman, M. A. Depressive affect and vulnerability to environmental change in the aged. In F. C. Jeffers (Ed.), *Duke University Council on Gerontology. Proceedings of seminars 1961-65.* Durham, N. C.: Regional Center for Study of Aging, Duke University, 1965, 328-335.

Lippincott, R. C. Depressive illness. Identification and treatment in the elderly. *Geriatrics,* 1968, *23,* 149-152.

McKinley, C. K. & Dreisbach, L. K. Variations in depressive symptomatology as a function of age. *Texas Reports on Biology and Medicine,* 1967, *25,* 179-185.

Menninger, K. A. Old age without depression — a personal view. *Medical World News,* 1971, (Spec. Issue — *Geriatrics*), 64-65; 71.

Morozova, T. N. & Shumskii, N. G. (The clinical picture of involutional melancholia and its relationship to the age factor.) *Zhurnal Neuropatologii i Psikhiatrii,* 1966, *66*, 598-604.

Myler, B. B. Depression and death in the aged. Unpublished doctoral dissertation, Boston University, 1967. (*Dissertation Abstracts International,* 1967, *28*, 2146B.)

Nodine, J. H., Mapp, Y. J., Slap, J. W. & Siegler, P. E. Depression in geriatric practice. *Geriatrics,* 1963, *18*, 429-431.

Patterson, R. D. Grief and depression in old people. *Maryland Medical Journal,* 1969, *18*, 75-79.

Pergola, F. & Sireix, D. W. (Clinical aspects of depressive states in the aged.) *Prensa Médica Argentina,* 1971, *58*, 531-534.

Post, F. Depressive reactions in the elderly; a re-appraisal. *Gerontologist,* 1963, *3*, 156-159.

Post, F. Diagnosis and prognosis of depression. In W. F. Anderson & B. Isaacs (Eds.), *Current achievements in geriatrics.* London: Cassell, 1964, 178-183.

Post, F. The management and nature of depressive illnesses in late life: A follow-through study. *British Journal of Psychiatry,* 1972, *121*, 393-404.

Rondepierre, J. J. (Depressive psychoses in aged persons.) *Revue Pratique,* 1963, *13*, 3045-3052.

Rosenthal, S. H. Recognition of depression. *Geriatrics,* 1968, *23*, 111-115.

Rothman, I. Depression in the older patient. *Journal of the American College of Neuropsychiatry,* 1962, *1*, 45-51.

Sarteschi, P., Cassano, G. B., Castrogiovanni, P. & Conti, L. Studio degli aspetti psicopatologici delle psiconevrosi e delle sindromi depressive endogene dell'età senile, mediante analisi multivariate. *Giornale di Gerontologia,* 1972, *20*, 935-952.

Schwab, J. J., Brown, J. M., & Holzer, C. E. Sex and age differences in depression in medical in-patients. A preliminary report. *Mental Hygiene,* 1968, 52, 627-638.

Shternberg, E. Y. & Rokhlina, M. L. (Some general clinical features of depressions in later years.) *Zhurnal Neuropatologii i Psikhiatrii,* 1970, 70, 1356-1364.

Shumskii, N. G. (Melancholy states in old age with Cotard's syndrome.) *Zhurnal Neuropatologii i Psikhiatrii,* 1962, 62, 1536-1543.

da Silva, G. The loneliness and death of an old man. Three years' psychotherapy of an eighty-one-year-old depressed patient. *Journal of Geriatric Psychiatry,* 1968, 1, 5-27.

Smith, D. H. Depression in the aged. *West Virginia Medical Journal,* 1965, 61, 334-336.

Stenback, A. On involutional and middle age depressions. *Acta Psychiatrica Scandinavica,* 1963, 39 (Suppl. 169), 14-32.

Stenback, A. Objects loss and depression; with special reference to aging. *Archives of General Psychiatry,* 1965, 12, 144-151.

Verwoerdt, A. & Dovenmuehle, R. H. Physical illness and depressive symptomatology. *Journal of Gerontology,* 1964, 19, 330-335.

Weckowicz, T. E., Nutter, R. W., Cruise, D. G., et al. Speed in test performance in relation to depressive illness and age. *Journal of the Canadian Psychiatric Association,* 1972, 17 (Suppl. 2), SS241.

Weissman, M. M., Paykel, E. S., Siegel, R., & Klerman, G. L. The social role performance of depressed women: Comparisons with a normal group. *American Journal of Orthopsychiatry,* 1971, 41, 390-405.

Weitbrecht, H. I. (Chronic depression.) *Wiener Zeitschrift für Nervenheilkunde und Deren Grenzgebiete,* 1967, 24, 265-281.

Wilson, L. A. & Lawson, I. R. Situational depression in the elderly; a study of 23 cases. *Gerontologia Clinica,* 1962, 4 (Suppl.), 59-71.

Wilson, L. A. Situational depression in geriatric patients. *Medical News,* February, 1965, 6.

Wolff, K. Depression and suicide in the geriatric patient. *Journal of the American Geriatrics Society,* 1969, *17,* 668-672.

Zacher, A. N. Goal rigidity as a variable in mid-life and old age depression. Unpublished doctoral dissertation, Washington University St. Louis, 1971. (*Dissertation Abstracts International,* 1971, *32,* 1230B.)

Zung, W. W. Depression in the normal aged. *Psychosomatics,* 1967, *8,* 287-292.

Zung, W. W. Mood disturbances in the elderly. *Gerontologist,* 1970, *10,* 2-4.

VII. AFFECT

A. Affective Changes With Age

Borge, G. F., Buchsbaum, M., Goodwin, F., Murphy, D., & Silverman, J. Neuropsychological correlates of affective disorders. *Archives of General Psychiatry*, 1971, *24*, 501-504.

Daly, R. J. & Cochrane, C. M. Affective disorder taxonomies in middle-aged females. *British Journal of Psychiatry*, 1968, *114*, 1295-1297.

Dean, L. R. Aging and the decline of affect. *Journal of Gerontology*, 1962, *17*, 440-446.

Friedman, A. S. & Granick, S. A note on anger and aggression in old age. *Journal of Gerontology*, 1963, *18*, 283-285.

Lakin, M. & Eisdorfer, C. A study of affective expression among the aged. In C. Tibbitts & W. Donahue (Eds.), *Social and psychological aspects of aging*. New York: Columbia University Press, 1962, 650-654.

Llewellyn, C. E., Jr. Tranquility or hostility in senescence. *Psychosomatics*, 1968, *9* (Suppl.), 22-26.

Reiter, S. R. The relationship of angry and fearful behavior to perception among institutionalized geriatric residents. Unpublished doctoral dissertation, Columbia University, 1961. (*Dissertation Abstracts International*, 1961, *22*, 1719.)

Zung, W. W. K. Mood disturbances in the elderly. *Gerontologist*, 1970, *10*, 2-4.

B. Anxiety, Agitation, and Tension

Alder, J. Tension states in the aged and infirm. *Journal of the Tennessee Medical Association,* 1960, *53,* 1. (Abstract in *Journal of the American Geriatrics Society,* 1960, *8,* 736-737.

Birkmayer, W. & Danielczyk, W. (Agitation states in old age and their management.) *Wiener Medizinische Wochenschrift,* 1964, *114,* 490-492.

Claghorn, J. The many faces of anxiety in different age groups. *New York State Journal of Medicine,* 1971, *71,* 331-334.

Handal, P. J. The relationship between subjective life expectancy, death anxiety and general anxiety. *Journal of Clinical Psychology,* 1969, *25,* 39-42.

Krishna, K. P. A study of relationship between manifest anxiety and age. *Indian Journal of Gerontology,* 1971, *3,* 30-32.

Nagashima, K. (Study on personality traits and neurotic anxiety of aged.) *Acta Gerontologica Japonica* (Yokufuen Chosa Kenkyu Kiyo), 1968, *47,* 81-102. (English Abstract, p. 9.)

Templer, D. I. The construction and validation of a death anxiety scale. Unpublished doctoral dissertation, University of Kentucky, 1968.

Templer, D. I. Death anxiety as related to depression and health of retired persons. *Journal of Gerontology,* 1971, *26,* 521-523.

Vassiliou, V., Gerogas, J. G., & Vassiliou, G. Variations in manifest anxiety due to sex, age, and education. *Journal of Personality and Social Psychology,* 1967, *6,* 194-197.

Ytrehus, A. (Treatment of anxiety states in the aged.) *Tidsskrift for den Norske Laegenforening,* 1967, *87,* 1495-1497.

VIII. MENTAL CONFUSION

Anonymous. Old age, nutrition, and mental confusion. *British Medical Journal*, 1969, *3*, 608-609.

Brocklehurst, J. C. Mental confusion. *Nursing Times*, 1967, *63*, 937-938.

Craigie, H., Robinson, R. A., Henderson, J. H., et al. The confused elderly. *Health Bulletin*, 1969, *27*, 9-16.

Graux, P., Lelievre, A., & Desan, J. (Senile mental confusion.) *Maroc Médical*, 1968, *48*, 280-284.

Hendrickx, J. (Reversible confusional states in the aged.) *Tijdschrift voor Sociale Geneeskunde*, 1969, *25*, 195-200. (Abstract in *Excerpta Medica*, Sect. 20, 1970, *13*, 288.)

Kataria, M. S. Confusion in the elderly; language of disordered function. *Medical World*, 1969, *107*, 17-20.

Lawson, I. R. Confusion in the house; the assessment of disorientation for the familar in the home. *Psychiatric Quarterly*, 1969, *43*, 225-239. (*Psychological Abstracts*, 1970, *44*, 15217.)

MacDonell, J. A. The anatomy of confusion. *Manitoba Medical Revue*, 1962, *42*, 293-295. (Abstract in *Excerpta Medica*, Sect. 20, 1962, *5*, 1562.)

Macrae, A. K. M. & Craigie, H. The confused elderly. *Health Bulletin*, 1969, *27*, 9-16. (Abstract in *Excerpta Medica*, Sect. 20, 1970, *13*, 292.)

McDonald, C. Psychogeriatric confusion. Studied under control and prospectively. *Geriatrics*, 1968, *23*, 178-182.

Murphy, E. The confused elderly patient. *Journal of the Irish Medical Association*, 1968, *61*, 99-103.

Nobbs, K. L. Confusion in the elderly. *Nursing Times*, 1962, *58*, 1190-1192.

Patrick, M. L. Care of the confused elderly patient. *American Journal of Nursing*, 1967, *67*, 2536-2539.

Stork-Groenveld, I. & Meerloo, J. A. (Acute mental confusion in elderly.) *Praxis*, 1971, *60*, 844-847.

Weinberg, J. Understanding mentally confused elderly persons. *Postgraduate Medicine*, 1970, *47*, 116-119.

Wolff, K. The confused geriatric patient. *Journal of the American Geriatrics Society*, 1964, *12*, 266-270.

THE ETHEL PERCY ANDRUS GERONTOLOGY CENTER

The Gerontology Center was established in 1964 for the purpose of creating a special environment for training and research in human development and aging. In 1971 it became the Ethel Percy Andrus Gerontology Center in honor of the founder of the National Retired Teacher's Association, The American Association of Retired Persons and an alumna of the University of Southern California.

Over 400,000 members of the organizations founded by Dr. Andrus contributed generously toward the construction of the 88,000 square foot, three story brick building on the west side of the campus. Alumni, philanthropic foundations and friends of USC also contributed substantially to the establishment of the Andrus Center, which was dedicated in February, 1973.

The operations of the Andrus Center may be divided into three principal areas:

1. The Research Institute initiates, designs, and executes research on the many phases of aging.
2. Community Programs is directed to the application and demonstration of the Center's research efforts.
3. The Leonard Davis School of Gerontology provides a curriculum for the undergraduate and graduate education and training of professional personnel to meet growing needs in the expanding field of aging.

The harmonious integration of these operations will contribute to progress in many directions in the years ahead.